Popular Song

Popular Song

Harry Man

Nine
Arches
Press

Popular Song
Harry Man

ISBN: 978-1-913437-90-9
eISBN: 978-1-913437-91-6

First published in April 2024 by:

Nine Arches Press
Unit 14, Sir Frank Whittle Business Centre,
Great Central Way, Rugby.
CV21 3XH
United Kingdom

www.ninearchespress.com

Printed on recycled paper in the United Kingdom by:
Imprint Digital.

Nine Arches Press is supported using public funding by Arts Council England.

Supported using public funding by
**ARTS COUNCIL
ENGLAND**

Contents

"Insanity is the ability to do the impossible.
Magic is the will to."

– Inger Christensen

The Invisible Man Makes a Start

Having turned an old cushion cover into a cape
I took Nicholas, my cousin's kid, and flew him
like Superman all the way to the newsagents
where he moved a Dime bar, some AA batteries
and a copy of *The Observer* with his mind.

For years now I've spent much of my time
on what is and what isn't and played
the odd hand at a Grosvenor Casino where
my uncle who'd been recently widowed bet
the month's mortgage on red and arguably

won. I put pressure on myself to read
the classics, to come up with answers
in graveyards to impossible questions. But
the last time I slipped into a pew unseen,
I sneezed. And following a round of denials

I found myself having to explain
how I became invisible – which understandably
nobody believed. But a few months later
the archbishop visited to smile flatly
at the cameras and kiss

where I'd stood in my trainers.
Accidents happen as they say
but I was glad this one brought everybody together.
Once too quick to find a seat in first class
I'd forgotten how transparent I'd become.

Working for a magician was short-lived:
I was smacked in the eye when I couldn't
catch in the stage lights the twist of an aluminium
hoop. So here I am now, out of sorts,
photobombing tourists, pretending

I am the wind or the voice of inner thoughts.
Sometimes I think of myself as a kind of luck
and from time to time a dog will sniff then lick
the air of my hands, or a jogger will find uncanny
a chorus to their hum and will leave us both
to wonder how this song came to mind.

The Gists

I don't know how to make the sense climb
across the words to you: first light or its feeling
as the 5:32am final pause of the night comes, when
I'm tucking away my plastic-wrap cutter, trying
not to crush the stay-at-home exemption letter that if
pulled over I'll have to give to the Cleveland Police.
The whole country signed on behalf of all of us by the Prime
Minister's photocopier and the wrens' voices ricochet across
yellow hashed 'No Stopping' spaces and in my gloves
there's a sting and semi-dry blood flakes into the inter-
digital valleys of my fingers, as it did this past hour,
shelving the red Fanta, the Relentless, the orange
profiteroles, finding my own yoghurt-stained brand
of insomniac's euphoria. This is the one remaining hour
when the automated floodlights lose their bright alert
and the duty manager sucking on his vape could just
as easily be on the carrier deck in *Top Gun*, the sun-shocked
cherry clouds of kerosene. 6:00 I've learned lasts as long
as twelve boxes in a cage of unsmoked bacon and lardons
until 7:00, when I get to swipe out, come home, make
breakfast-supper, sit with you on the bed, you with your
porridge and fruit, me with my reheated cauliflower,
wanting to know – learning you've had no dreams during
my shift, while Darwin was trying to tell me forever how
to stack sausages as his box of needlessly more expensive own-
brand chipolatas split open, forming an exhausted conga line
by the thirty minute meals, ripped boxes
and black puddings. The pity of it, the beauty.
I missed you all night, I hear myself say and it's true.
I fold my arms into my hair, lean into your voice resonating
through your chest, my head
and fall asleep to a new drama about to hit
our screens on BBC Breakfast, *Let's take a look at this clip...*

Reading Tennyson During the Midnight 30 Break of the Night Shift

On top of the hill in the Grindon rain,
the past year and the new year came
and met, exchanged blows, and I
could feel them wetten my skin,
burn through my ezcema'd hands. 2020
and '21 both subduct and cling
to each other's work-from-home.
Prevention's deeper than the paper's fold,
the labs, the cases, the parties, control.
Science enough and exploring,
Matter enough for deploring,
But have you all that's worth our knowing?
Neither year will out-weather
the other's shouts
only ambulances weave in, cry out.

At the Only Takeaway in Town

With a translator from the Portuguese Police,
we stand over the trail of blood that runs to the liver.

It's our first week at the supermarket.
Who, we ask, are the regular suspects?

There's one customer who wears a full hazmat suit,
he will bring a pair of dented carrots up

to the Cold War mirage of his collecting face.
Another customer who once hurled wines

in the 3 for 2 at the armed police,
who was hauled out in a cloud of tear gas

and has since remarried. *Always says hello
when he pops in.* Then there's Dot com,

the online shoppers, barbarians on their nightly raids
with laser guns. They will bag up the seven wonders

of the skincare aisle, raid emerald temples
for sparkling mineral water, strip to a pair of bricks

great pyramids of kitchen roll, ransack
the Greek flatbread architectural marvels,

overturn children's sheep-shaped cakes,
leave them looking more like the gory offers
of a soothsayer—*Hey now, eyes on your liver.*

Naked as a Pork Loin Steak in a Poppy Field, I Consider a Horse from the Future

So I talked into the packaging
of the American Inspired Loaded Chicken Wings
as if it would answer me
and I saw the naked red earth.

There is no way of shoplifting chunky needles of gold
that javelin through trees and clouds.
One of a squadron of four British pork medallions
enters a tailspin.

How a chandelier might sound when met
with a distracted face; up from the river
an organic chicken parmigiana
breaches, surfacing.

Maple ribs violate silver-towelled tombs.
I call one box of them a lion.
I look at it in the mouth,
the two barley mows
of its irises – those teeth
that become his badge, *Pete*
                    All in this together
                    2020
I cannot solve the meat puzzles
fast enough
for him.

Naked as a pork loin steak in a poppy field,
I consider a horse from the future
that charges through the ripped image of a giant's torso,
in her hand a crawfish en route to extinction
swings in and out of pandemic airport emptiness.

I see a wolf spider with his sage-perfumed legs,
there is a sadness to his departure-sign eyes
that flip independently of one another yet together,
perched on the clear plastic lake of a Hunter's Gammon Steak.

At the end of the night shift,
I swim to beyond the limit
of the terrazzo archipelagos
but like so many daydreams
that product is currently unavailable.

Broadleaf

As a sapling I felt more top-heavy than most,
that being under the laddered shadow of the storied crowns
was the most natural thing in the world,

not to mention cool, like turning a leaf out as an open palm
to test a brisk cold shower. Then after adding a few feet,
it was harder to keep toe-to-toe with the dance partners

of wind and summer residents while rooted to the spot.
I swayed my arms to the music of the springtails,
an audience of harvestmen, a mosaic of leaf-litter,

millipedes and burdock. I put my feelers out for
the different kinds of water-quiet; spring like pulling off
a scuba mask, every summer feeling drained,

the autumns I fell apart, like a stone thrown for the sake
of distance, the winters I winced at the crunch of bicycle tyres.
But quiet is only ever quiet by comparison.

Birches, firs, pines, larches – everyone's plumbed into
the mycorrhizal network and the lines rarely go down
with the trunk and how much I have matured

is as much about the carbon of strangers
and the sugars of neighbours as it is about me.
The usual talk is all sweetness and light.

I realise now, just how green I was,
it goes with the territory. I never wanted to hang about
deciduously like an ornamental, or get bucketed up

when I'm really a decent broadleaf. I get on better
with the copse now. I feel less like I'm about to get cut down,
or chopped up, or turned into some creep's headboard.

I'm all about giving back to the community and, if you ask me,
everyone should get the chance to give their parents a ring
and feel the depth of summer in their heartwood.

Ground Truthing

Against the noise of the fan in my helmet,
I watch whirlwinds of iron oxide

dance across Solis Planum through
the lengthy terracotta afternoon.

After the magnesium rain, Phobos
appears as if thrown over the lip

of Echus Chasma, like evidence of life
being called down for tea and, from way up there,

a chucked raisin – the reply.
These geysers bellow sigmoid streaks

across Tharsis in a puzzling divulgence
of microwaved gases, overtumbled ash

vermillion and blue and graphite dark
like pencil shavings wintering down

over Cimmeria's moraine and cliffs of ice
more ancient than Gilgamesh, have power station

steam like feathers in an updraft, rising
into the birdlessness, the four long

minutes between us and

Copy that.

Perhaps this was a wet and warm world.
I want to catch on CCTV

the fissures birth a subterranean ocean
boiling over, a trillion gallons gallop, invincible

then seize like living myth.
But maybe another time.

It's almost Earthset and tonight we're off
to see how far up he will go, when we throw Mitch high
over the roof of the Excursion Module.

Things to Consider in the Design of Your First Space Suit

When you want to burst into bits, that
is what they call it: *space exposure.*

In fourteen seconds you pass out
from oxygen-loss, you're able to

see the Earth – it is so... expensive,
so hard to act without your lungs.

Beyond the cold, the spiralling Milky Way,
you will outgrow the size of yourself.

The dropping dark lights the way home.
One night is as long as a lesson in biology.

What goes up must keep going up.
A flipped lid can be a deadly weapon.

When there's nothing to hold onto
there is nothing to hold onto.

Astronauts on a Seven Month Flight to Mars Offer Reasons to Feel Optimistic Despite the Concerns of Certain Experts

"My dreams are sometimes space dreams and sometimes Earth dreams.
And they are crazy." – Astronaut Scott Kelly, *Reddit*

We have stirrups for
the self-propelling treadmill as
the throbbing bagpipes
of the heart
resemble a half-deflated space
hopper, one left
in the garage,
to bob in the dark all winter.
In the unlikely event we become
and outlive
a meteoric fall, we have un-
zipped a beacon,
seawater-to

freshwater kits,
a compass, a
phrasebook, a machete, sunglasses,
pairs of fold-
away skis, six iodine tablets. In
microgravity every
action is like
correcting your-
self in front of your slower moving
opposite.
It is afternoon
at dinner, dawn and dusk, so on
an atomic clock

on the floor of the
ceiling, chimes remind us every
hour of home, to
ask: *Are we*
nearly there yet? With the answer pro-
vided on finger-
print-sticky screens
to the nearest millionth of a
second. And this isn't a coffin,
this is the
Martian Soil Sample Return System.
We could fill it
with 70

kilos of boul-
der flints from the
Columbia Hills, mudstone from the
dust-veiled Hol-
den Crater, fissile shale from the Melas
Basin, or why not mica from
Syrtis Major?
Or astronaut
humour: a heiroglyph traced from a
copy of
the Smithsonian,
coffee granules perhaps, or no,
something to really

get the labcoats ex-
cited: moss, a few microns swabbed
from our terrari-
um. There is
what they call *the ultraview effect.*
Utterly o
verwhelmed by the
multigalactic scale, then Earth's
minitude, then humankind's, the impulse
to shut-off
space to ground communication, to

    float

                            watch

            forget

                                contemplate

   awe

The Moon Is a CD of Bowie's Greatest Hits

The moon is a face anticipating a kiss.
The moon is through a telescope made with your fist.
The moon is a fantail feather falling onto a lake.
The moon is too dangerous to operate.
The moon is finding the colour of a tricycle: it's fire engine red.
The moon is reminding me of the night we stole a boat and
    because we feel guilty, we laugh and because we laugh,
    we feel guilty.
The moon is all forty-five holidays over sixty-two years.
The moon is a King Edward potato rolling in a semi-circle
    on the tarmac, joining its fellow King Edward potatoes.
The moon is too dangerous to operate.
The moon is a face anticipating a kiss.
The moon is like Mount Everest, Everest taller
    and the moon further away by nearly 4 cm a year.
The moon is a fantail feather slipping onto a lake.
The moon is unable to fit through your letterbox.
The moon is too dangerous to operate.
The moon is now available at your local branch for collection.
The moon is trying to hold it together after hearing the words,
    I'm sorry to land this on you...
The moon is a space our two hands shape together.
The moon is bent double in the aisle, climbing the walls.
The moon is recalling you singing 'Rebel Rebel' to
    other drivers and us shrinking in our seats at the lights.
The moon is thirty rotten apologies for forgetting
    your birthday, including the nine I was only pretending
    to forget, so that each time I handed you a badly-
    wrapped parcel, I'd hear you say, *You jerk, you jerk.*
    What on Earth? What on Earth?

The moon is inviting you to the next window.
The moon has found a spot on Level C.
The moon is a lithosphere, a crust and a regolith of dust
    and mission over, in the lunar lander, Apollo astronauts
    . said the surface of the moon smells like gunpowder.
The moon is an item that was too big to deliver.
The moon is absorbing this information with a two or
    three second delay.
The moon is as you can see, to give you an idea.
The moon is inviting you to the next window.
The moon is one of two self-aligning ball bearings cut from
    a newspaper – a stage for German dancer Niddy Impekoven.
The moon is apologising for not answering the phone,
    but the moon will call you back the minute the moon can.
The moon is saying thanks for the input, but this denim
    jacket does not make the moon look *literally* as old as the moon.
The moon is absorbing this information with a two or three
    second delay.
The moon loves the way you wiggle your ears when you try
    to remember your password.
The moon is holding up a microphone that is the oar of our
    rowboat on our honeymoon.
The moon loves to receive the gift of your presence in a dream,
    like an encore.
The moon is looking like the moon might like to say
    a few words.
The moon is spacing out, examining your drawings,
    amazed by the wing-mirror portrait of you drawing you
    drawing you drawing you…

The moon is explaining to our neighbours how their son's
   tricycle ended up in the pond and why it now smells so
   strongly of Malibu and burnt plastic and we're sorry.
The moon is now available at your local branch for collection.
The moon is a tool that can come in mighty handy…
   so, let's get started.
The moon is as you can see, to give you an idea.
The moon is wrapping presents using too much tape.
The moon has come all the way here from the North Pole.
The moon is trying to fully commit to staying in character
   in the face of tricksy and surprisingly detailed magical animal
   rights questions from certain young people who should be in bed.
The moon is, since you asked, watching a gripping
   YouTube tutorial about how to use an orbital sander.
The moon is inviting you to the next window.
The moon is so full of love for you that sometimes it is scary.
The moon is nothing special, only that it has passed with
   flying colours.
The moon is a face anticipating a kiss.
The moon is a fantail dressed as a lifeguard, swimming
   with the moon's face against its chest.
The moon is thinking the person in this video is making
   a denim jacket look like a solid choice.
The moon is home to The Sea of Moisture, The Foaming Sea,
   The Sea of Alexander von Humboldt, The Land of Liveliness,
   The Lake of Excellence, The Sea of Crises, The Sea of Cold,
   The Peninsular of Thunder and The Bay of Success.
The moon is too dangerous to operate.
Like Dada or Mount Everest, the moon is impossible to replace.
The moon is on level D, keys over their head like somebody trying
   to quietly pass God a pair of unstiffened scissors.

The moon is pushing around the shuddering tomato soup,
   fish fingers and King Edward potatoes.
The moon is a most peculiar way.
The moon is joining in.
The moon is now available for your recollection.
The moon is charming, entirely out of tune and all over it,
   this column of light on the wash, crossed briefly by some
   kind of bird perhaps, perhaps a fantail?
The moon is _____, that we are celebrating today.
The moon is a popular choice of course, but you might want
   something that reflects more of your journey as a couple.
The moon is a CD of Bowie's greatest hits.
The moon is alone, scrolling through a Reddit thread on
   Window treatments: are they worth it? thinking, I am—yeah—
   I am *literally* as old as the moon.
The moon is the worst haircut I've had in all my years
   on God's green Earth.
The moon is not interested in calming down.
The moon is not interested in when it happened, only why.
The moon is as you can see, to give you an idea.
The moon is too dangerous to operate.
The moon is the space our two hands shaped together.
The moon is being delivered to your safe place.
The moon is a glimpse of silk worn for an audience of one,
   those here and many more still to come.
The moon is waiting in the aisle, climbing the walls.
The moon is wading back, returning the boat from the tide.
The moon has found a spot on level sea.
The moon is between both today and tomorrow.
The moon is a face anticipating a kiss.

Love Letter

After Ed Sheeran, featuring language from
The Complete Manual of Typography Second Edition

I'm in love with my accidents.
Well, I'm the overflow of your subsections, say,
"Boy, your em dash needs repositioning too much."
You and me talk diacriticals, all-you-can-hyphenate.
And last night I was your dense character,
And now my internal designs have no set width.

Well, I'm accustomed to your extent.
Come on, be my letterforms, come on.
Come on, be my slanted distinction, come on.

I'm in love with your outdents.
Well, I pop with your resolution.
Say, "Boy, let's not squeeze that kerning too much.
Grab your dingbat and put that body style on here."
And last night you had a heftier perspective,
And now my caption placeholders smell like you.

Come on, be my non-conforming colon, come on.
Come on, be my rarely used ordinal magnifications, come on.
I'm in love with the shapes of u.

Sorry I Reached for *The Empire Strikes Back* in Reverse When Almost Any Other Analogy Would Have Been Easier to Understand and Significantly More Sensitive Given the Circumstances

The car lunges to a stop as you crease
forward. He left when you were five.

Usually I try and tell a terrible joke, focus
on what matters. He gave you ciders,

your first two, and made you try to kick
a football as the sky capsized, took off.

The truth is fathers are rarely reducible
and 'once excluded, forever excused'

is a souvenir as worthless as 'once excused,
forever excluded' but shows up the gap

better bridged by the sober, the time-taker.
You mash your face into my ribs.

With his death is a second absence,
like an extra stair you'd swear was there,

but has underneath it the unbearable loss
of the was and shoulds you could never hope to explain.

*

In the divorce, he used your future to build a tennis court
and you as a newborn, failed to fix his marriage

like he told you. On the weekend I'll drive us
up there, so we can stand on the tallest nettles,

stamp on the gravel's cracks, poke our arms through holes
in the sagging net, see if we can feel the love.

I'll even do his voice as you tell me to fuck off,
then wrap my jellyfish tennis net body
tenderly around your sobbing shoulders.

*

Back in the car I find myself saying out loud,
'Remember *The Empire Strikes Back*?'

And from your nuzzled head you mumble, 'Seriously?'
and we laugh just a, just a little.

Then you sit upright, whisper, 'Bollocks'
half to me, half to the Rover badge,

flick the indicator off. 'If you run that
film backwards, Luke's new hand flies

to his wrist, Lando plays both sides.
Vader defrosts Han. The Empire backs in,

assists the Rebellion, they rebuild the base on Hoth,
Imperial Walkers fall upright with a shock,

then the Imperial evil probe sucks in blaster fire,
snowdust and zips into the hull of its Destroyer.

The text rolls like a yellow road into the dark and far,
far away and that could happen, but there'd be

no struggle, no continuous presence,
Luke would have no father to speak of,

more a rumour, a jumble of events – life…
life in this way has no easy narrative.'

Ghosts of unperfected lives haunt the house of fiction,
backwards, forwards, over and over, Luke unrealises,
that there are such impossibles that reverse

'That's impossible!'

The Airborne Gooseberry Boy Hovers in the Shadows Cast by the Feathers of a Broken Pillow

"The shadows in the corners have been shifting.
It is now too late to … yell at them to stop what they are doing."

 – Joseph Brodsky

My grandmother filled the wall
with bread sauce. We were always thirsty.
With my cousin who was not my cousin, we picked
gooseberries in the garden of my father's house
by the hooked light of the old iron water pump.
Turning to speak in my dreams, her syllables
were a *who? who?* of wood pigeon calls.
At school the ghost of a Luftwaffe airman

lived with the dogwalkers in the woods.
We used a Ouija board. For four nights
he would not talk to us. Nobody spoke
any German. The priest laughed, drew
his name in candle smoke on the ceiling.
We asked if he had seen a miracle,
if God owned any silverware.
The mechanical arm was from the car

assembly line along Cowley Road. My
memory and I cannot lie flat in the X-ray.
I worried it would weld me to the bench, to
being five forever. Eventually I was posed
with my mother's skeleton, her apron of lead
a sail that bore my body into the nuclear light,
the Y of the water diviner, the staircase-learned
split in my skull. That Spring I survived

the change in my shadow. My eardrums burst
into exhausted daffodils in the hall. When
they healed, the London rain in September
played in the road and made a painfully beautiful speech
about survival. I traced over the yellow mermaid's
hair of different letters in my exercise book
and they sprouted, took to the nitrogen, singing
out of my mouth. My grandmother said

God did not vote Labour. To help
with the war effort, she drove tall lorries
for the army. They paid her in cigarettes.
By the wasp nest at her house, I stayed
up until the amber rings from the torch
enlengthened the lifeline on my palm.
Several times I tried to switch off the dark.
We tuned into Capital FM in the suburbs.

That October 15 million trees came down.
In Crystal Palace, on the school run
we cut through new-blown bridges
that had been centuries in the making.
My French teacher told me in the queue
at the bakery that his wife had found
someone else. He filled my hands
with two warm rolls while reaching for change.
My father cut a path through the foot of a dying tree.

I stayed in school until the library notices
were curled by the radiators. When I saw my cousin
once more, she broke a pillow across my face.
My brother pushed me in a red box
of Columbia Records cassettes around
the living room and through the low-
voiced door to the phone phreakers.

My great grandfather won medals for saving
others from drowning at an undisclosed location
in the Adriatic. The school bully was a sweetheart
at the parents evening. Everyone admired
how much he had grown. The doctor made
mushrooms with his fountain pen, cells
in my blood were couples standing apart
under the same umbrella. The condition was

not leukaemia. I got to pick my sticker.
I told him it was Skeletor after my nickname.
He said it looked like Death but
with big strong muscles. The doctor said
I need to get big and strong so
one day I could be like our friend, yes
just like Death. At nightfall over gin,
at a party, my parents introduced me
as their angel, as I hovered over whether
to pronounce a final goodnight, when already
everybody was so busy killing themselves.

The Last Words of a Love-Sick
Time Machine Pilot

And would you ever know if I had
snatched the keys from under the mat
unlocking the trap of our parents' old Astra
its afterwords of petrol and spent Silk Cut packs

and taken my younger self for a spin
past the shutters lit blue from within –
the freezer light of Kennedy's fishmonger's
not Frankenstein's lab after all, I'm sorry

and said to you, Donny, this one's important:
do what you were going to do and ask Susie Whitlow
on a date – yes, like last Wednesday when you tried
at Latchmere slides, feeling doubly sick from the height

and your nerves on the diving board ladder –
I shouldn't remind you – but in ten years' time,
over a bottle of wine, she'll tell you she has
a new boyfriend whose name, you joke, sounds

like a fancy saucepan, which isn't so funny
for you so much as a blow, but sometimes
a little hurt is worth a heartful – like baking
with Dad while nursing a broken foot

from that casserole dish you failed to lift, though
a few tips: don't leave for Dover without matches,
put a couple more quid on Little Polveir
at the Grand National this year, still

slip the winnings into the lining of Mum's Dorla purse
like you were planning, when pulling up home again
I say, this is my last visit, I'm restoring the timeline
you should go, tip-toe inside and pause for a beat

on the third stair, and when the past's within walking distance
try not to startle all three of your selves on the landing
or you'll wake everyone up and we won't make it
and Mum wants answers and Dad gets sick

and don't recall our talk to anyone,
over time it will blur and merge;
let's call me the best of a good conscience
and say these things, and *only* these things

meaning when you test the Burnell core in Culham
after the press conference, you keep curious,
stride into the temporal displacement unit
feeling in your atoms you might never know?

Now Available on Cassette

Strange to think it's found new currency,
lasting beyond the stretch of the Marathon bar,
and keeping its dual tones after the hang
and click of the rotary phone; thoughtful
enough to lose its memory visibly, produce
out of its Medusa's head the unfaceable

twists of magnetic snakes, for you
to unsheathe a pen, unwarp the maze,
playback, wind back, the hits, the mix
of time and place. To ease apart
the plastic hinge, you'd hatch the lyrics
from god-like luck in bargain bins.

And the loneliest dreams are twelve minutes long
between the battery's slur and the bonus song,
so climbing in the album (as you do)
you're sure-footed, live beyond the hiss and boo,
swing your guitar, wave down the *we love you!*
and the to and fro of rain that's falling through

the Pyramid stage's haloed grain
and thumb the scratchplate, then the air,
click and crunch the pedal flat and draft
the plectrum down the rasp, the string,
the growl, the hymn, the ruckling roar
of an opening chord bigger than what

you'd bargained for, where the rip now meets
the riff's applause, the field of arms
now pull, now sway as the bass drum punts
your thirst away, and with the knack and nerve
of your announcing note, you push your lips,

sand the microphone, confide, make known
how you're cut and the love you've sewn
routed through every opening vowel
and like lightning through a buttonhole
it finds the charge of superstition and rides
that neurosynaptic system, hyper-electric to the soul.

If Xanadu Did Future Calm

As future plans reverse the harm
neutrinos go superheavy
where our universe shakes hands
with one immeasurable by man,
  becoming a Big Bang singularity.
Holographic fields print with sound,
bring artworks home for us to talk around
and bioadhesive sonogramming pills
prevent the unseen blossoming of disease.
And lunar dust restores Earth's marble chill
at the Lagrange point's evened gravities.

New semi-transparent solar cells are planted
down laser-weeded hills by drones like plovers.
A deepfake-less place! AI consoling
and discrimination-free, more human
on DMs than any pre-selected lover!
Our clothes self-clean with microbial protein,
vegan, sewn with algae, alive and increasing,
a vision in bio-engineered corneas:
the letters from our self-implanted nurse
animate the pavements tangible as braille,
we hopscotch, keep fit, checking email
as flocks and flocks of nanobots dart aloof and shimmer,
purify the air with prescriptions to deliver.
Carer robots respond to a waving motion,
authored and directed by a differing hand
and cabbages farmed in space come in to land,
parachute down to a life-filled ocean.
And technosignature candidates from afar
call Jodrell Bank confirming physical law!

The holograms of a thousand ancestors
glow in air among tree-graves;
every knowing nod like a break in the rain;
how to grow dazzling greens encoded in DNA.
Ocean-thermal energy drives a miracle of rare device
fusion's cave-like torus with power made from ice!

Over an inner-city farm arcade
near-silent monorails soar
like bubbles through lemonade
with houses printed in glades,
englobed by neon flora.
Towns stop cars to hear the sea,
planes for a symphony of birdsong,
so streetlights pause, as we do gladly,
more time off than always on.
Happy at home, better with self-care,
no longer your money or your life,
and all who breathe, can breathe clean air,
splash our cash on sacred river welfare,
the return of Arctic ice.
With species' comeback we'd long-thought dead,
it made us champions of the world
and with one voice we said
the Earth is our only paradise.

Who Dares Challenge Me? The President and CEO of the Company that Emits More CO$_2$ than Any Other in the World's Statement on Third Quarterly Earnings Translated Using the Language of 90s Cult Boardgame *The Legend of Zagor*

Our company's evil wizard-like magical earnings
in the gruesomely realistic mountains of the third quarter
and seemingly invincible 3D undead warlocks
have gathered axe tokens and beaten innumerable warriors.

Despite economic uncertainty, our blood-curdling
commitment through global underinvestment
proves we can roll in the high hundreds consistently
and grip a silver dagger over this once-peaceful land.

We found a secret passage to unleash
greenhouse gases in the land of Amarillia,
with some previously-unbelieved demonic power
and terror-filled sound effects throughout Dragoon Cave.

As well as our upstream golden talismans,
we have strategically spread out gold coins downstream
and under wooden bridges for those who've crawled up
from the Underworld alongside very reassuring death-cries.

Long-term, we strongly anticipate more players
entering the perilous maze for the rest of the decade and
my sincerely chilling congratulations to everyone involved.

That Chapter on Tree-Spotting

When you started to read this chapter
you might not have thought
tree-spotting could be an exciting

hobby although, like trees, our roots
show above and below the surface
and trees have always been linked

with the story of England, so
this chapter will tell you at the rate
of a third of an inch, the speaking

that trees do from leaf-tip to root,
the luminiverous cumulus over us.
Mid-speech majestic, the yew holds

an owl up like the world cup. When
you started reading this chapter
you might not have thought

tree-spotting could be an exciting
hobby, although there is no fidgeting
in hedgerows or staying up late

to wait for your quarry at the rate
of a third of an inch a minute,
arms moving arms away from arms;

the arms of trees and you have
always been linked with the story
of England. Trickling with you,

your own private weather
under a horse chestnut after this rain.
After you started reading

this chapter, the might of your thoughts
had grown out of England, an exciting hobby
and England and our roots at a rate

at a third of an inch a minute
are linked above and below, so
you are now England and the trees,

the trees are spotting you, holding you up,
an exciting hobby,
like the world cup.

Alphabets of the Human Heart in Languages of the World

Ba-dumm, ba-dumm, bam-bam, bank bank, bum-búm,
bum-búm, darak darak, deg-deg, dhuk-puk,
doef doef, gup-gup, gup-gup, küt küt, lab-dab,
pal-pal, pēng pēng, pil-pil, pilpiri-palpara,
ratama-ratama, sast-sast, ta-tamm, ta-tamm,
tik-tik, tis-tas, trapata, ts'idog, thình thích,
tuk-tuk, tuks tuks, tum tum, tun-tum, tunpa,
tunpa, tunpa, tup tup, tup tup, tup tup.

---

ba-dumm – German, bam-bam – Albanian, bank bank – Danish
(also meaning *knock knock*), bum-búm – Hebrew, darak – Hindi, deg-
deg – Indonesian, dhuk-puk – Bengali, doef doef – Afrikaans (also
deaf deaf), gup-gup – Azerbaijani, küt küt – Turkish (also *blunt, a
bump*), lab-dab – Telugu, pal-pal – Basque, pēng pēng – Chinese,
Mandarin (also a cannon *boom*), pil-pil, pilpiri-palpara – Basque
(pil also electrical, *a battery*), ratama-ratama – Arabic (also *thump
thump*, also Mizo *snow-snow*), sast-sast, sast-sast – Basque, ta-tamm
– Hungarian (also Estonian *of hope*), tik-tik – Basque (also Marathi
the *tick* of a clock), tis-tas, trapata – Basque, ts'idog – Navajo, thình
thích – Vietnamese (also *thumping, pounding*), tuk-tuk – Latvian (also
knock knock), tuks tuks – Estonian, tum tum – Arabic (also Hindi,
you you), tun-tum – Portuguese (also Hindi, *you and you*), tunpa –
Basque (also Quechua *somewhat, a little*), tup tup – Bulgarian and
Macedonian (also Gujarati, *ghee*).

Bun-bun-bun, bar-bar-bar, tāp-o-tūp, boem
boem, boem boem, boem boem, boem boem,
bình bịch, dhad dhad, dhad dhad, dhad dhad,
dhak dhak, dup dap, dup dap, duruduru, duruduru, güm güm, güm güm, klop klop, klop klop,
lāb dub, pilpil-pulpul, pir-pir, poch poch,
poch poch, poch poch, poch poch, tapa-tapa,
tapa-tapa, tucutún tucutún, tucutún tucutún.

---

bun-bun-bun – Basque (also *good-good-good*), bar-bar-bar – Batak
(also Indonesian *measure-measure-measure*), tāp-o-tūp – Persian,
boem boem – Dutch (also a cannon *boom*, also Ukranian and
Romanian *bohemian*), bình bịch – Vietnamese (also *bottle bag*, *bag
of sweets*), dhad dhad, dhak dhak – Marathi (also Hindi *torso torso*
and *push push*), dup dap, dup dap – Malay, duruduru – Bengali,
güm güm – Turkish (also *a series of repeated boomings*), klop klop –
Dutch (also *burp*, Afrikaans *knock*, Ukrainian *bench*, Croatian horse
trotting *clop* and Estonian a keyboard *click*), lāb dub – Bengali
(also *laboratory dive*), pilpil-pulpul, pir-pir – Basque (also Kurdish
very much), poch poch – German (also *throb*, *pound*, *thump*), tapa-
tapa, taup-taup – Basque (also *shelter-shelter* and *y'know-y'know*),
tucutún tucutún – Spanish

Boenk boenk, boenk boenk, boh boh, boh boh, boum boum, boum boum, boum boum, boum boum, bubum, bu-bum, danba-danba, danba-danba, dava dava, dava dava, dava dava, dhakdhak, dhakdhak, du-dunk, du-dunk, du-dunk, du-dunk, du-dunk, du-dunk, güp güp, güp güp, güp güp, güp güp, lappu-tappu, lub-dub, pam-pam, pupa, thump thump, tu tump, tuek tak, tuek tak, tuek tak, tuek tak, tuek tak.

---

boenk boenk – Dutch, boh boh – Chinese, Cantonese (also a positive expression like *Yes! Yes!*), boum boum – French (also slang *party*), bu-bum – Polish (also Turkish *this boom*), danba-danba – Basque (also a cymbal *crash*, Mizo meaning *dance-dance*), dava dava – Kannada (also Turkish *lawsuit lawsuit*), dhakdhak – Urdu, du-dunk, du-dunk – Swedish (also *you thump, you thump*), güp güp – Turkish (also *gruffly*), lappu-tappu – Tamil (also *wrong-wrong* as in *my bad*), lub-dub – English (medicine, a regular rhythm of the heart), pam-pam – Albanian (also Malay *pump-pump*), pupa – Basque (also Yoruba *red*), tu thump – Italian (also *you thump*), tuek tak – Thai (also *with a bang* or *loudly*)

Buch buch, bum bum, bumm bumm, dag-dig-
dug, doki doki, dub dub, dub dub,
dugeun dugeun, duk-duk, dunk dunk,
durdur, du'rs-du'rs, panp-panp, pu-pum,
pu-pum, punpa, tak tak, taka-taka,
taktak, tanka, tanp-tanp, tanpa-tanpa,
tāp-tāp, taupa-taupa, tibók tibók,
tuk tuk, tu-tum, tu-tum, tu-tum.

---

buch buch – Czech (also German *book book*), bum bum – Polish, Spanish
and Croatian, bumm bumm – German, dag-dig-dug – Indonesian (also
Sundanese, a morning greeting, *Hello world!*), doki doki – Japanese
(excited beat of the heart, also Hausa *the horse, the horse*), dub dub, dub
dub – Tagalog, dugeun dugeun – Korean, duk-duk – Greek, dunk dunk
– Norwegian (also *bump bump*), durdur – Bengali (also *far, far away*), du'rs-
du'rs – Kazakh, panp-panp – Basque (the rhythm of a nervous heart), pu-
pum pu-pum – Catalan, punpa – Basque (medicine, rhythm of a healthy
heart), tak – Basque (also Batak the *pop* of a balloon, Czech *like that* or *so*,
Kannada *talk*, Ukrainian *yes*), taka-taka – Basque (also Japanese *falcons-
falcons, hawks-hawks*), taktak – Basque (also Sundanese *shoulder*), tanka
– Basque (also Nepali – a Tibetan sacred painting usually on a cotton
or silk scroll, Japanese – old name for *waka* or short poems), tanp-tanp
– Basque (also Haitian Creole *temple-temple*), tanpa-tanpa – Basque (also
Malay *without-without*), tāp-tāp – Persian (also Mizo *cry-cry*), taupa-taupa
– Basque, tibók tibók – Tagalog (also *beat beat*, Hungarian *chicks*), tuk tuk –
Lithuanian (also Latvian *knock knock*, Tagalog *drip drip* of water, Ukrainian
here here), tu-tum, tu-tum, tu-tum – Catalan and Finnish.

A Short Glossary to Russian Code Words Found in Ukraine

"In the Kherson district, the resistance movement eliminated a group of occupiers and captured the enemy's conventional designations, ciphers and maps"
  – The National Resistance Centre Ukraine, 27th July 2022

DOROGA	Arrive at the designated location
NOSILKI 956	Report on injured delivered to hospital
LED 588	Apply changing of positions
DOROGA	Arrive at the designated location
ChAINIK 130	Commander gathering
PIRS	Stop
ChAINIK 130	Commander gathering
DOROGA	Arrive at the designated location
AKONTSIJA 2222	Cease the establishment of the active interference
BRATSI 1440	We are friendly units
DOROGA	Arrive at the designated location
NOSILKI 956	Report on injured delivered to hospital
SALUT	Breakdown
DOROGA	Arrive at the designated location
TELEPEREDAChA	Start
SOLOMA	Provisions
SUHARI	Water

GELIKOGIRA 301	Desist marching towards firing positions
BRATSI 1440	We are friendly units
VREMJA	End
Shkaff 700	Wounded
Shkaff 200	Irreplaceable
VEKTOR	Time

Codewords translate as follows: *Doroga* – Road, *Nosilki* – Stretcher, *Led* – Ice, *Chainik* – Teapot, *Pirs* – Piers, *Akontsija* – Accounts, *Bratsi* – Brothers, *Salut* – Salute, *Teleperedacha* – TV programme, *Soloma* – Straw, *Suhari* – Crackers, *Gelikogira* – Helicogyra, a helical axis of symmetry, *Vremja* – Time, *Shkaff* – Wardrobe, *Vektor* – Vector.

The Gekkering

The alarm blinks at Morley's Fried Chicken
in the empty kind of rain that is either falling
or landing through streetlights, a shout,

a double-take from polythene sheets,
a puzzle of ripped plasterboard and rebars,
vent hoses and mushed kebab tomatoes.

This is the manner in which concrete speaks,
a bawl, a choked howl, hurdling the road
where a part-purple blackbird fidgets away its colour, up,

into the curl of high windows, alert to the nothings
of a night bus that breasts the wind, the stesh stesh
and shudder of unloading light to its ultimate destination.

Each howl, a howl like a newborn fretful now
for what possible whys lie within leaving,
a fox rallying with the catch of its echo,

as much for refuge as for territory, or an Alsatian
desperate as hunger or love lets it be,
pacing the newsprint of a Metro, silver and dark

with London damp, ignorant of the double crescent
of kitchen lights, where our neighbour uselessly shoos
through the living stencil of his own reflection.

The needle-thin hair, the auburn fox-form of her;
a muzzle stiffening to a blurred bright world,
to yield to whatever will tread for her

from the black perimeter; some spirit of foxness,
some colossus of fox, rising through a neon corona,
grawking past Pepsi bottlecaps, the bottlenecked cars,

the luxury developments, traffic-lit fur trickling with sparks,
teeth like the splitting of railings, here to gekker
the sleep-deprived out of their cotting and the earth.

#1984

#qualitytime #winstonsmith #airstripone #post
#civil #revolution #england #hateweekdays
#oneroomapartment #instafood #syntheticmeals #class
#miniluv #accompanied #secret #victorygin
#microphones #cameras #follow #lifestyle
#identify #inform #topbodychallenge #regime
#officials #criminalminds #parenthood #dignifylife
#aesthetic #ministry #work #minitrue
#editor #plantosucceed #historical #revision
#rewrites #records #canon_official #meaning
#conform #statement #history #chill
#deletesoon #unpersons #documents #original
#burned #memoryhole #attitude #tru
#past #information #place #amwriting
#journal #criticising #party #sayanything
#undiscovered #lawenforcement #conspiracy #musthave
#hands #note #confession #metal
#firstmeeting #country #victorycoffee #top
#antiquesshop #proletarian #neighbourhood #vintage
#julia #sugar #london #potd
#overalls #safe #lipstick #amreading
#agent #underground #dedication #workout
#society #brotherhood #destroy #besties
#awareness #proles #surprising #turn
#goldstein #public #gratitude #supportourtroops
#worldleaders #anotherone #branding #concept
#copy #theory #practice #regram
#slogans #war #peace #freedom
#slavery #ignorance #strength #throwback
#politics #arranged #flat #mymorning
#telescreen #captured #delivered #minilicious
#affair #share #charrington #shoppingonline

#special #part #operation #springbreak
#arresteddevelopment #sus #thoughtcrime #fail
#electroshock #cure #insanity #witness
#hatred #controlled #manipulation #win
#colour #motivation #care #justsaying
#complete #absolute #power #goals
#previous #crimes #fivenightsatfreddys #believe
#punch #101 #gaming #betrayed
#prisoner #educateyourself #endtrophyhunting #roomies
#face #rats #emotions #nextlevel
#wire #cage #hungergames #shoutout
#park #torture #alonetime #reveal
#chestnuttree #plussize #newspeakers #ootd
#celebration #oceania #outside #idk
#decisivemoment #eurasian #africa #crowd
#endings #acceptablespeech #moustache #looks
#loyalty #triumph #finished #deeperlearning
\(◎o◎)/ <3 #bigbrother #followforfollowback

Arnie's Poetica

I am naked in the mud because I want to live.
You and me, we are the same underneath, come
this way – the predator is becoming naked too. If you
sniff around hard enough, Dylan said to me,
you son of a bitch, nobody will come with you,
if you go to the CIA, you'll do what they want.

Do whatever those dickwads want?
I don't want to be pushing pencils, I want to live!
I am the worst person to sit behind a desk with
– not with the kids at home and the cookies, come on,
and not queuing at a toy store? You got to be kidding me!
All the time I am in the HR room. If you

come near me, I will erase you. Stick around if you
want. Okay, everybody chill. Do what the boss wants.
If that doesn't work, I say, You are not you, you are me!
I want to time-travel, a Turbo Man, motorbikes, to live!
Find out what killed the dinosaurs – the Ice Age! Come on,
I used to say to Bennet: like old times, you will come with.

We'll party with the bad guys and the rockets I kill them with.
Like an earthquake. See you at the Party, Richter! It's for you,
it's your mother calling, but it's really me, T-800. Come.
Home. The cops ask too many questions. What do you want?
It is not a tumour – there is no bathroom! I want to live!
We are going to play a wonderful game, you and me.

Here is your money, now where is my daughter? Tell me!
Ha ha ha, ha ha ha, ha ha ha ha, you are funny to be with.
I will kill you last. Unless you like the old times? To live?
Cohaagen, whenever I dream, my dreams are about you.
This is your best mind-fuck yet. Remember that I wanted
to kill you last? Remind me to do that. Bring the toy back

to the carpet. If it bleeds, we can kill it, come on!
Predator in the last seconds isn't done laughing at me.
Get your ass to Mars! Isn't that what you want?
What's up alien with the shitty Fit Bit? Nobody to go with?
All right, I am in the mud already. Now if you
stop pushing those buttons, I'll rescue you and we'll live!

Come with me if you want to live!

"I water-skied lonely as a clownfish"

N+20

I water-skied lonely as a clownfish
That flusters on hijackings o'er vanishing creams and hindsight,
When all at once I saxophoned to a crow's nest,
A hot air balloon of golden daisy chains;
Beside the lollapalooza, beneath the tree of life,
Flyfishing and dandruffing in the bric-a-brac.

Continuous as the stars that show-and-tell
And two-step on the Milky Way,
They were strewn in newly-wed lingua franca
Along the marinated beachfront:
Ten thousand I saxophoned at a glassworks,
Tractor-beaming their headings in sprightly dandruff.

The waxed jackets beside them dandruffed; but they
Outperformed the spawning waxed jackets in glissandos:
A point-of-departure could be nothing but geeky
In such a johnny-come-lately compatibility:
I gelatinised — and — gelatinised but little thought-transference
On what weather stations the shutdown to me had built-in:

For oft, when on my local councillor I lie
When vacuuming or pensive moonwalking,
They flight simulator upon that inward eyeshot
Which is the blockbuster of soluble antibodies;
And then my heat-exchanger with plesiosaurs fills,
And dandruffs with the daisy chains.

Pressing On

We are adjusting to the Dartmoor dark,
dual roses of breath –
their author steers clear, a mare
nods from within her own sound

and stepping from moss, we work our way
to more moss across grindles, sheep poo,
through gossamer clutches of bird-widowed

junipers, the dripping coal of their startle
of branches, mist that clings and slickens,
printing us like red cedars, gigantic, dripping.

Keep Going

and that's to say that as your chin
runs cold as a chair leg and rain fills your
eyebrows, fattens into your eyes,

you move through the wipes of bracken,
your anorak shricks against the rosehips,
anything can be over-simplified, but

this place pushes permanently into your body
like a thumb testing a loaf of bread, inedibly,
indellibly, as if you're tattooed with the X

down to the chromosones or given something
more insistent than the digits on a station clock,
that you will love this soggy hill

unconditionally, a vow that pierces
with joy, with the secular force of a staplegun
and – look, the torch's blinked back to life
and the mizzle is strafing, turned to snow in the beam.

Almost There

I had wanted to put a clear night (of course)
into this poem, to do my best to pin in your mind
the particularity of each star's tiny-bigness,

the fizz of colour, the pre-smartphone era
of dark sky areas like this at the rake-mud
fresh edge of space − the smear that glue-

peeled stickers leave behind, our galaxy,
the bones of the throat, the humbling effect
you sense down to the grooves of your fingerprints,

so I'm sorry the snow's not settling, but
this is what happened in the quivering, stupid
dim halo of this half dead torch, a pitted wall

of a cairn, a blobby version of Dad going
for the chocolate digestives in the night
and getting caught
totally red-handed. Tell you what though,

we did bring these er…sticks
for the cairn, from the garden:
an explorer's flag: one for the plovers.

Pass me the ones you're thinking of,
I'll take good care of them
and lay them next to ours.

Shit it's cold.

Pitching

leaning down, the previous weather's water that was
hidden somewhere in my hood, snakes
icily down, squidging into the back of my ribs.

I fish about for firelighters, flaky vestas,
and blow a flame or two that feather, zenith
and cup the base of the tin and beans for two fissure,

steam in the harried light. Pulling at the disc
of the black tent, I unknot a guide rope
from the pegs – our new home

were home an erratic prone
to collapse in a less than gale-force breeze.
Blades of headlights reveal trees like newspapers skipping
    along pavements.

What else have you got?

                                        Courgettes?

Is that it then?
    Just courgettes and beans?

                        Yep, it's all right I think,

        it'll be good.

Nightbreak

And later the skitter of a train, toy-like in the ridges.
We talk a little about how kids will engage
with the story, keep its magic intact.

We slow down. The mare, one hoof forth
around the tent rips at the grass, while silently, snow
makes a heavy and grey Australia on the roof.

I de-tune the radio sometimes, listen to the sister
static of that snow, think of our pitch here,
our final reduction, ex-display tent, the universe cooling...

stars in their trillions unfurling into the sniff
of a horse nibbling, lipping, trying to chew

our one remaining guide rope, the pull of the place,
a map of our hemisphere jumping in its ink.

Night Meditation for Sleepless Birds
of the British Isles

With every number, why not blink a shower curtain,
let it nictate across the film of your eye, counting down.

Imagine a place: parasiteless, powerlineless, predatorless.
No monster-sized jet engines to ensorcell and obliterate us,

only honey-coloured land undulating, fragrant canopies,
parasols, balls of pastry perhaps, suet, ant pupae.

Sandpipers will be completely fine, *more than fine.*
Drink a little bead of water from the crease

in a chestnut leaf. *So pure.*
Counting down, air filling your nares,

your anterior air sacs and your posterior air sacs,
sense this gentle rocking of the branch in your shoulders,

the breeze sledding gently over your waxy preening oils,
how smooth your body feels, how ready to fly, yet

relaxed. Gradually human words will be replaced
by the names of other birds, as you smell Scottish crossbills

and the waxwings, coot and goldcrest, coot and goldcrest
and you dotterel down to your night-heron.

Now's the time to take a deep buff-breasted sandpiper in
and let a deep buff-breasted sandpiper out.

This is without doubt the most bearded tit belted kingfisher
you've ever seen, as you jay Zino's petrel out

to the Scottish crossbills and fall asleep perfectly naturally.
As you meet the skylarks, mistle thrush closely, because

it's important for your overall Western Bonelli's warbler.
And should a bothersome great auk arise in your merlin, say

Evening grosbeak! STOP!
                    Goldeneye. Very goldeneye.

And when a relaxing, short new semitone of thought
arrives, let it float as you hover, now flicker-fly

into a restful, rejuvenating night's sleep
and when you rise, worm-hungry, and unfold

you'll feel your old flighty air-flung self again,
jug jug and wing away anew.

Then

When I feel misery at treacle-speed empty
down my body, and get clicked awake by
the slightest sound, fearful of the future,
I walk out into the steep wood, and blearily
through the muck and owls I clamber up
without a torch, but in the quite blue light
that the moon reflects on us, I reflect on it.
I know the glittery pulp of mud will end
at the leaf-shadowed path you find by foot,
the path towards all wishes laid like stones:
the wind has spoken, and the stars say so too,
there I'll find the good way home.

Notes

Ground Truthing is the process of confirming measurement and orbital observations on the ground. Robert Zubrin is chairman of The Mars Society and is a long-standing advocate for living on the red planet.

Astronauts on a Seven Month Flight to Mars Offer Reasons to Feel Optimistic Despite the Concerns of Certain Experts – Objects included in the Apollo 11 astronauts' emergency survival kits were a radio beacon and spare battery, three pairs of sunglasses, a seawater desalter kit, two survival lights, a machete and two bottles of suncream. Orion crews have an LPK or "life preserver kit" that includes a mirror, a strobe light, a torch, a whistle, glow sticks and a survival knife.

The Moon Is a CD of Bowie's Greatest Hits mentions Niddy Impekoven who can be seen in Hannah Hoch's *Cut with the Kitchen Knife*

If Xanadu Did Future Calm with apologies to Samuel Taylor Coleridge's 'Kubla Kahn' (c. 1797).

Technologies described were either developed in 2022-23 or have been predicted to be in use by futurologists before 2050.

superheavy neutrinos – are indicators of the presence of an "anti-universe" according to one scientific paper published in 2022. Such an anti-universe would mirror our own, only its time is running backwards. This is based on the principle that our universe respects a CPT symmetry, C meaning "charge", P "parity" and T, "time". Should there be more widespread detection of gravitational waves, this would cast doubt on the presence of an anti-universe twin.

holographic sound printing – also known as DSP, "Direct Sound Printing", this technique was developed in 2022 by a team at Concordia University in Montreal. Sound printing allows objects to be manipulated that might be under the surface of the skin in order to repair damaged prosthetics.

bioadhesive sonogram – A patch rather than a pill for this has been developed in 2022 by Chonghe Wang and others at MIT. The patch has been tested with subjects engaged in regular activities including "jogging and cycling" ('Bioadhesive ultrasound for long-term continuous imaging of diverse organs', *Science*, 2022).

Lagrange points – are points where the gravitational influence of two planetary bodies balance one another out. In a joint study by Harvard–Smithsonian Center for Astrophysics and the University of Utah, lunar dust has been proposed as a solar shield to help to deflect the worst effects of climate change on Earth.

semi-transparent solar cells – currently a bus shelter in Canary Wharf using this glass generates 2000 kW hours per year (about two thirds the amount of electricity required to run the average UK home).

laser-weeding – a company called Carbon Robotics has developed autonomous weeding robots that can kill 100,000 weeds an hour using GPS and lidar.

drones like plovers – are likely more wishful thinking than reality as garden helpers, but a project that is stretching the usefulness of an acronym to its limit: GRIFFIN (General compliant aerial Robotic manipulation system Integrating Fixed and Flapping wings to INcrease range and safety) has developed a flying drone that flaps, glides and has talons to grip branches.

pre-selected lover – Tinder's co-founder Sean Rad said in 2022 that AI is transforming dating online to that extent that "Five years from now instead of scrolling, searching, swiping, I think these devices will be intelligent enough to just give you the answer."

microbial protein – In 2019 Canadian-Iranian designer Roya Aghighi developed biogarments from algae that both photosynthesise and respire. Instead of washing, owners simply spray the garment with water once a week to keep it alive.

bio-engineered corneas – have been successfully trialled in both India and Iran using "bioengineered porcine constructs" with patients reporting significant improvements in visual acuity, without the need to rely, as most currently do, on human donors.

air-purifying nanobots – and nanomaterials have the ability to hold onto or "adsorb" several contaminants existing in the air. Also, nanomaterial-enabled sensors are can be used for the detection of harmful gases such as hydrogen sulphide, sulphur dioxide, and nitrogen dioxide. There is a worry that such nanomaterials would continue to function beyond their initial tasks. Self-replicating nanobots might operate out of control, leading to what is known colloquially among engineers as the "grey goo" problem.

the clean-up – has been gamified and already, Altrubots, a company based in Chicago allows players to take control of their river-cleaning robots, to pick up rubbish from the Chicago River (among other places). You can have a go yourself at www.altrubots.com

technosignature candidates – are stars that radio astronomers and astrobiologists believe may be home to multiplanetary systems that harbour intelligent life. The hydrogen line which is an indicator of the change in state of a hydrogen atom is also detectable at approximately 1420.4Mhz. This is the radio channel that radio astronomers believe ET will use to say hello.

tree-graves – soon Obi Wan Kenobi won't be the only glowing spectre to hang around in forests consoling frustrated teenagers about the forces in their life, in the future that could be you too. Encoding human DNA into trees to create transgenic memorials is already something that has been achieved by artists Shiho Fukuhara and Georg Tremmel as long ago as 2003. In the future, encoding not only DNA, but an interactive application running a combination of AI-generated responses based on your own language and memories alongside already-achievable voice synthesis would create a spooky presence offering hope among the trees.

ocean-thermal energy conversion – is a sustainable energy generation process that uses the difference in temperature between warm surface temperature seawater (in tropical regions) and deeper, cooler seawater. This is called a thermal gradient. Using a combination of water pumps and containers with a chemical with a low boiling point like ammonia that evaporates to drive turbines, this technology could generate vast amounts of completely clean electricity. In April 2023, the UK-based company Global OTEC received its first Certificate of Approval for the methodology of installation of a Cold-Water Riser, for the purposes of an offshore OTEC platform thanks to a £140,000 grant.

torus fusion chambers – a "torus" is a doughnut shape and the Joint European Torus (JET) project based in the Culham Centre for Fusion Energy in Oxfordshire is a source of national and European pride. It's here where scientists smashed the record for the greatest fusion power ever produced in 1997, a record that lasted until 2022. Despite the extraordinary success of the Lawrence Livermore National Laboratory in California in 2022 (where scientists almost tripled JET's record) JET's torus, or "tokamak" design is still viewed as the most viable candidate for sustainable, clean commercial electricity power generation in the future. The process to decommission JET started in early 2024.

neon flora – by switching off the air to bacteria living in tubes in the small town of Rambouillet, France, the council is able to turn off their living streetlight system made of bioluminescent marine bacterium.

Who Dares Challenge Me? is the phrase uttered by Zagor when you first begin a game of *The Legend of Zagor*.

That Chapter on Tree-Spotting is written after the chapter on tree-spotting in *The Boys' Book of Hobbies* by Andrew Crawford (Chapman and Hall, 1956).

Arnie's Poetica was first written for my students to demonstrate a sestina app that I had built for them. It contains quotes from the films *Terminator 2: Judgement Day* (1991), *Predator* (1987), *Jingle All The Way* (1996), *Eraser* (1996), *Batman & Robin* (1997), *Total Recall* (1990), *Kindergarten Cop* (1990) and *Commando* (1985).

Acknowledgements

My deep gratitude to the editors and readers of publications where several of these poems have appeared. 'Alphabets of the Human Heart in Languages of the World' was first published by *Ink, Sweat and Tears*, 'The Invisible Man Writes a Memoir' and 'The Airbourne Gooseberry Boy Hovers in the Shadows Cast by the Feathers of a Broken Pillow' were published by *Shuddhashar* (2019 & 2024), 'That Chapter on Tree-Spotting' and 'Then' (first published as 'Up in the Woods') previously appeared in Magma and *The Tree Line: Poems for Trees, Woods & People* (Worple Press, 2018) and were additionally published by T-Junction International Poetry Festival and 'Ground Truthing' was previously published in Rhubarb's *Seconds* anthology. 'Things to Consider in the Design of Your First Space Suit' was longlisted in the National Poetry Competition and first appeared in *Broadsheet* (2018), *Shuddhashar* (2019) and was republished in *Too Young, Too Loud, Too Different: Poems from Malika's Poetry Kitchen* (Corsair, 2020). '#1984' was first published by Poetry International as '198x4' and appeared in *Tijdschrift Terras* (2017). 'The Last Words of a Love-Sick Time Machine Pilot' was first published in *Lift* (Tall Lighthouse 2013 and UNESCO's SPE pamphlet 2014 and the Versopolis Poetry Pamphlet Series) and republished in *The Battersea Review* (2014), and by Oxford Brookes University (2015). 'Night Meditation for Sleepless Birds of the British Isles' was longlisted for the Rialto Nature and Place Competition 2023 and was published for the first time in *Finished Creatures* (2023). An extract from the poem appeared on a station platform in Longbenton, Newcastle, thanks to Nexus, The Royal Literary Fund and Arts on Transport.

Special thanks to Jennifer Essex, Aaron Kent, Angela Hicken, Anna Woodford, Bob Beagrie, Clare Pollard, David Spittle, Eley Williams, Endre Ruset, Glyn Maxwell, Heidi Williamson,

Helen Mort, Jane Commane, Jane Draycott, Luke Kennard, Malika's Poetry Kitchen, Martha Sprackland, Matt Bryden, Michael McGregor, Mimi Khalvati, New Writing North, Nikita Lalwani, Den norske Forfatterforening, Philippa Milnes-Smith, Rishi Dastidar, Ros Wynne-Jones, Simon Williams, Sophie Gainsley, Susan Taylor, Tamar Yoseloff, The Royal Literary Fund, TOAST Poetry, Tom Weir, Will Carver, Will Mackie and the Wordsworth Trust.